D1304143

The Bake Sale Cookbook

The Bake Sale Cookbook

A fantastic collection of 80 recipes for
best-selling favorites

This edition published in 2012
LOVE FOOD is an imprint of Parragon Books Ltd

Parragon
Queen Street House
4 Queen Street
Bath BA1 1HE, UK

Copyright © Parragon Books Ltd 2011

LOVE FOOD and the accompanying heart device is a registered trademark of
Parragon Books Ltd in Australia, the UK, USA, India, and the EU.

www.parragon.com

All rights reserved. No part of this publication may be reproduced, stored in a retrieval
system, or transmitted, in any form or by any means, electronic, mechanical, photocopying,
recording, or otherwise, without the prior permission of the copyright holder.

ISBN: 978-1-4454-8200-2

Printed in China

Cover design by Talking Design

Notes for the Reader
This book uses standard kitchen measuring spoons and cups. All spoon and cup
measurements are level unless otherwise indicated. Unless otherwise stated, milk is assumed
to be whole, eggs are large, individual vegetables are medium, and pepper is freshly ground
black pepper. Unless otherwise stated, all root vegetables should be washed and peeled
before using.

The times given are only an approximate guide. Preparation times differ according to the
techniques used by different people and the cooking times may also vary from those given.
Optional ingredients, variations, or serving suggestions have not been included in the
calculations.

Recipes using raw or very lightly cooked eggs should be avoided by infants, the elderly,
pregnant women, and anyone with a chronic illness. Pregnant and breast-feeding women
are advised to avoid eating peanuts and peanut products. People with nut allergies should
be aware that some of the prepared ingredients used in the recipes in this book may contain
nuts. Always check the packaging before use.

CONTENTS

INTRODUCTION

Bake sales are a great way to make money for a worthwhile cause, whether it's your scout troop, a local charitable organization, or a response to a national disaster. Bake sales bring people together, reinforcing the neighborhood sense of community. Apart from that, they're a boon to busy moms with little time to bake, and could even be said to provide a service to the community — everyone loves a sweet treat every now and then!

Planning a bake sale can be plenty of fun, but there's also a lot of hard work involved. Follow our handy tips and you'll be sure to have a successful sale.

Don't do it alone

It doesn't matter how organized a person you are, you cannot plan and run a successful bake sale without help—a lot of help. Everything that needs to be done can be delegated, so put those organizational skills to use by recruiting a volunteer force from friends, family, and the wider community. You'll need volunteers to organize publicity, set up the booth, sell goods on the day, collect donations, and clean up at the end of the sale. Most importantly, you'll need an army of willing bakers! Make sure everyone is clear about what they should be doing and follow up with them on a regular basis. You can get the kids involved as well—they can design posters, labels, cake banners, and decals, and even bake simple cakes and cookies under supervision.

Get things started

Draw up lists of the cookies and large cakes that will be needed for the sale and allocate bakers to make them. Be very specific about what is needed, otherwise you'll end up with a lot of chocolate cookies and cakes and not much else. Because of the prevalence of nut allergies, nuts should be avoided. Cakes with a fresh cream filling cannot be properly stored in a nonrefrigerated environment. You don't want to overwhelm your volunteers, so the general rule should be one batch of cookies or one large cake per person, and remember that baking large cakes is not a task for the novice baker. Some people will want to eat their purchases on the spot, so make sure you have a supply of paper plates, napkins, and plastic forks. You could sell coffee and/or cold beverages to help wash down the cakes, so come prepared with a coffee maker, plastic cups, and a cooler full of canned beverages or even some homemade lemonade.

Put the word out

Design some eye-catching flyers to put on community bulletin boards and distribute throughout your neighborhood. Ask store owners to display them in their windows. Post notices on social networking sites. Make sure to mention the date, time, place, and the cause being supported by the sale.

Location, location

Hold your bake sale in a location where you'll be noticed. That way you'll get a lot of passing trade from people who may have missed your advertising. Make sure that it is legal to hold a bake sale at your chosen venue, and that you have any appropriate permissions in place before you start organizing. A lot of schools are now actively discouraging bake sales because of the high-calorie content of baked goods, so don't assume that you'll automatically get permission to hold a sale on school premises.

Set up properly

Make sure you've got everything in place before the bake sale starts and there's a rush for the goodies at your booth. You will need:

- Folding tables & chairs
- An awning to protect against extremes of weather
- A tablecloth and some decorations
- Trash can and garbage bags
- Cash box with enough money to provide change
- Cooler and ice if you're going to sell drinks
- Paper plates, napkins, forks, and plastic cups for those who want to eat on the spot
- A jar for contributions from people who don't want to buy a cake or cookies, but would like to donate some cash

Know your customers

If you're expecting a lot of moms and dads to visit your bake sale, make sure to have plenty of whole cakes and cookies by the dozen because they are likely to want to stock up on goodies to feed the whole family or even to freeze for another day. If, on the other hand, you'll be selling to small children or seniors, it's a good idea to package cookies or muffins individually—not everyone will be able to afford a whole batch. Consider including some wholesome options, such as low-fat muffins and oat bars, for the health conscious.

Wrap it up!

Packaging is very important for the sake of hygiene and presentation. Consult your state's health code for pointers on wrapping baked goods for sale to the public. At the very least, all of the goods should be protected from prodding fingers, flies, etc. It's a good idea to supply your bakers with some packaging, usually clear or printed cellophane bags (available from party goods stores or on the Internet) and ribbon. The bags can be fastened with fun decals (avoid staples, which can cut fingers). The labels in the back of this book can be cut out, filled in, and attached to the bags with lengths of pretty ribbon. Likewise, the banners can be cut out, filled in, attached to toothpicks, and stuck into the larger cakes. It's a good idea to add a label listing the ingredients on each package, especially potential food allergens, such as nuts, wheat, dairy, eggs, coconut, and fruits.

Cakes & Pies

Pound Cake

Serves 8–10

¾ cup unsalted butter,
   plus extra for greasing
scant 1 cup superfine sugar
finely grated rind of 1 lemon
3 extra large eggs, beaten
1 cup all-purpose flour
1 cup self-rising flour
2–3 tbsp brandy or milk
2 slices of citron peel

Preheat the oven to 325°F/160°C. Grease and line a 7-inch/18-cm round, deep cake pan.

Cream together the butter and sugar until pale and fluffy.

Add the lemon rind and gradually beat in the eggs. Sift in the flours and fold in evenly, adding enough brandy to make a soft consistency.

Spoon the batter into the prepared pan and smooth level. Lay the slices of citron peel on top of the cake.

Bake in the preheated oven for 1–1¼ hours, or until well risen, golden brown, and springy to the touch.

Cool in the pan for 10 minutes, then turn out and cool completely on a wire rack.

variation
omit the citron peel, brush the cooked cake with honey, and top with candied fruit

Raspberry Sponge Cake

Serves 8–10

¾ cup unsalted butter, softened,
   plus extra for greasing

¾ cup superfine sugar

3 eggs, beaten

scant 1½ cups self-rising flour

pinch of salt

3 tbsp raspberry jelly

1 tbsp confectioners' sugar

Preheat the oven to 350°F/180°C. Grease and line the bottoms of two 8-inch/20-cm round layer cake pans.

Cream together the butter and superfine sugar together until pale and fluffy. Gradually add the eggs, beating well after each addition. Sift in the flour and salt and fold in evenly with a metal spoon.

Divide the batter between the prepared pans and smooth level. Bake in the preheated oven for 25–30 minutes, until well risen, golden brown, and beginning to shrink away from the sides of the pans.

Remove from the oven and let stand for 1 minute. Loosen the cakes from around the edge of the pans, then turn out and cool completely on a wire rack.

When completely cool, sandwich the cakes together with the jelly and dust with the confectioners' sugar.

Cinnamon Swirl Bundt Cake

Serves 8–10

¾ cup unsalted butter,
   plus extra for greasing

1½ cups superfine sugar

3 eggs, beaten

1 cup sour cream

1 tsp vanilla extract

2½ cups all-purpose flour,
   plus extra for dusting

1 tsp baking powder

1 tsp baking soda

½ tsp salt

½ cup chopped walnuts
   (optional)

Swirl

1 tbsp ground cinnamon

3 tbsp light brown sugar

2 tbsp granulated sugar

Glaze

1 cup confectioners' sugar

about 1½ tbsp milk

1 tsp ground cinnamon,
   or to taste

Preheat the oven to 350°F/180°C. Grease a 10-inch/25-cm Bundt cake pan and dust with flour.

Cream together the butter and superfine sugar until pale and fluffy. Gradually add in the eggs, beating well after each addition. Beat in the sour cream and vanilla extract until well mixed. Sift in the flour, baking powder, baking soda, and salt, then mix until just combined. Stir in the walnuts, if using.

Pour half the batter into the prepared pan and spread evenly. Mix together all the ingredients for the swirl in a small bowl. Sprinkle the swirl evenly around the center of the cake batter, then cover with the remaining cake batter.

Bake in the preheated oven for 50 minutes, until a skewer inserted into the center of the cake comes out clean. Let cool in the pan for 20 minutes before turning out.

For the glaze, sift the confectioners' sugar into a small bowl and stir in enough of the milk to make a thick glaze with a pouring consistency. Stir in the cinnamon, then drizzle the glaze over the top of the cake. Let set.

Devil's Food Cake

Serves 8–10

5 oz/140 g semisweet chocolate,
 broken into pieces

scant ½ cup milk

2 tbsp unsweetened cocoa

⅔ cup unsalted butter, plus extra
 for greasing

⅔ cup light brown sugar

3 eggs, separated

4 tbsp sour cream

1¾ cups all-purpose flour

1 tsp baking soda

Frosting

5 oz/140 g semisweet chocolate,
 broken into pieces

⅓ cup unsweetened cocoa

4 tbsp sour cream

1 tbsp light corn syrup

3 tbsp unsalted butter

4 tbsp water

1¾ cups confectioners' sugar

Preheat the oven to 325°F/160°C. Grease and line the bottoms of two 8-inch/20-cm round layer cake pans. Place the chocolate, milk, and cocoa in a heatproof bowl over a saucepan of hot water, then heat gently, stirring, until melted and smooth.

Cream together the butter and brown sugar until pale and fluffy. Beat in the egg yolks, then the sour cream and the chocolate mixture. Sift in the flour and baking soda, then fold in evenly. In a separate bowl, whisk the egg whites until holding firm peaks. Fold into the batter lightly and evenly.

Divide the batter between the prepared pans. Bake in the preheated oven for 35–40 minutes, or until risen and firm to the touch. Let cool in the pans for 10 minutes, then turn out onto a wire rack.

For the frosting, place the chocolate, cocoa, sour cream, corn syrup, butter, and water in a saucepan and heat gently until melted. Remove from the heat and sift in the confectioners' sugar, stirring until smooth. Let cool until the mixture begins to thicken. Split the cakes in half to make four layers, then sandwich together with one-third of the frosting. Spread the remaining frosting over the top and sides of the cake.

Classic Cherry Cake

Serves 8

generous 1 cup candied cherries,
   quartered

¾ cup ground almonds

1¾ cups all-purpose flour

1 tsp baking powder

scant 1 cup unsalted butter,
   plus extra for greasing

1 cup superfine sugar

3 extra large eggs

juice and finely grated rind of
   1 lemon

6 sugar cubes, crushed

Preheat the oven to 350°F/180°C. Grease and line an 8-inch/20-cm round cake pan.

Stir together the candied cherries, ground almonds, and 1 tablespoon of the flour. Sift the remaining flour into a separate bowl with the baking powder.

Cream together the butter and superfine sugar until pale and fluffy. Gradually add the eggs, beating well after each addition.

Add the flour mixture and fold lightly and evenly into the creamed mixture with a metal spoon. Add the cherry mixture and fold in evenly. Finally, fold in the lemon juice and rind.

Spoon the batter into the prepared pan and sprinkle with the crushed sugar cubes. Bake in the preheated oven for 1–1¼ hours, or until risen, golden brown, and beginning to shrink away from the sides of the pan.

Cool in the pan for about 15 minutes, then turn out and cool completely on a wire rack.

Coffee & Walnut Cake

Serves 8

¾ cup unsalted butter,
  plus extra for greasing

¾ cup light brown sugar

3 extra large eggs, beaten

3 tbsp strong black coffee

1½ cups self-rising flour

1½ tsp baking powder

1 cup chopped walnuts

walnut halves, to decorate

Frosting

½ cup unsalted butter

1¾ cups confectioners' sugar

1 tbsp strong black coffee

½ tsp vanilla extract

Preheat the oven to 350°F/180°C. Grease and line the bottoms of two 8-inch/20-cm round layer cake pans.

Cream together the butter and brown sugar until pale and fluffy. Gradually add the eggs, beating well after each addition. Beat in the coffee.

Sift the flour and baking powder into the mixture, then fold in lightly and evenly with a metal spoon. Fold in the chopped walnuts.

Divide the batter between the prepared pans and smooth level. Bake in the preheated oven for 20–25 minutes, or until golden brown and springy to the touch. Turn out onto a wire rack to cool.

For the frosting, beat together the butter, confectioners' sugar, coffee, and vanilla extract, mixing until smooth and creamy.

Use about half of the frosting to sandwich the cakes together, then spread the remaining frosting on top and swirl with a metal spatula. Decorate with walnut halves.

Country Fruit Cake

Serves 10

1½ cups all-purpose flour

⅔ cup whole wheat flour

2 tsp baking powder

½ tsp ground nutmeg

¾ cup unsalted butter, softened,
    plus extra for greasing

generous ¾ cup light brown sugar

3 eggs, beaten

1 tsp vanilla extract

1 tbsp milk

1⅓ cups mixed dried fruit

1 tbsp raw brown sugar

Preheat the oven to 325°F/160°C. Grease and line an 8-inch/20-cm round, deep cake pan.

Sift the flours, baking powder, and nutmeg into a large bowl, adding any bran left in the sifter. Add the butter, light brown sugar, eggs, and vanilla extract. Beat well until is smooth, then stir in the milk and mixed dried fruit.

Spoon the batter into the prepared pan and smooth level. Sprinkle the raw brown sugar evenly over the surface. Bake in the preheated oven for 1 hour 20 minutes– 1 hour 30 minutes, or until risen, firm, and golden brown.

Let cool in the pan for about 20 minutes, then turn out and cool completely on a wire rack.

great tip!
stop the dried fruit from sinking by tossing with a little flour before using

Carrot Cake with Cream Cheese Frosting

Serves 8

2 cups all-purpose flour

1 tsp salt

2 tsp baking powder

1 tsp baking soda

2 tsp ground cinnamon

½ tsp ground ginger

2 cups superfine sugar

1¼ cups vegetable oil

4 eggs

4 tbsp melted unsalted butter,
   plus extra for greasing

2 cups grated carrots

225 g/8 oz canned crushed
   pineapple, drained

½ cup chopped pecans

½ cup chopped walnuts

store-bought carrot decorations,
   to decorate

Frosting

½ cup unsalted butter, softened

1 cup cream cheese, softened

1 tbsp milk

1 tsp vanilla extract

4 cups confectioners' sugar

Preheat the oven to 350°F/180°C. Lightly grease a 13 x 9-inch/33 x 23-cm baking dish.

Sift together the flour, salt, baking powder, baking soda, cinnamon, and ginger into a bowl and set aside.

Beat together the superfine sugar, oil, and eggs in a separate bowl until thoroughly combined. Beat in the melted butter. Stir in the carrots, pineapple, and nuts with a spatula, then stir in the flour mixture in two batches.

Spoon the batter into the prepared dish. Bake in the preheated oven for 40 minutes, until risen and firm to the touch. Let cool completely in the dish before frosting.

For the frosting, using an electric mixer, beat together the butter, cream cheese, milk, and vanilla extract until light and fluffy. Gradually beat in the confectioners' sugar until smooth. Spread the frosting evenly over the cooled cake and top each portion with a carrot decoration.

Banana Nut Bread

Serves 6–8

2 cups all-purpose flour,
   plus extra for dusting

1 tsp salt

1 tsp baking powder

1 tsp baking soda

½ cup unsalted butter, softened,
   plus extra for greasing

1 cup granulated sugar

2 eggs

1½ cups mashed banana
   (about 3 bananas)

1 cup chopped walnuts

2 tbsp milk

Preheat the oven to 325°F/160°C. Grease and lightly flour a 9 x 5 x 3-inch/ 23 x 13 x 8-cm loaf pan.

Sift together the flour, salt, baking powder, and baking soda into a bowl and set aside.

Cream together the butter and sugar in a separate bowl until pale and fluffy. Gradually add the eggs, beating well after each addition. Stir in the bananas, walnuts, and milk until thoroughly mixed. Add the flour mixture, stirring until just combined.

Spoon the batter into the prepared pan. Bake in the preheated oven for 1 hour 10 minutes, until a skewer inserted into the center comes out clean. Let cool in the pan for 20 minutes before turning out.

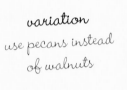

variation
use pecans instead
of walnuts

Coconut Cake

Serves 10

1¼ cups unsalted butter, softened, plus extra for greasing

scant 1 cup superfine sugar

3 eggs

1¼ cups self-rising flour

1½ tsp baking powder

½ tsp freshly grated nutmeg

⅔ cup dry unsweetened coconut

5 tbsp coconut cream

2¾ cups confectioners' sugar

5 tbsp pineapple jelly

toasted dry unsweetened coconut, to decorate

Preheat the oven to 350°F/180°C. Grease and line the bottoms of two 8-inch/20-cm round layer cake pans.

Place ¾ cup of the butter in a bowl with the superfine sugar and eggs and sift in the flour, baking powder, and nutmeg. Beat together until smooth, then stir in the coconut and 2 tablespoons of the coconut cream.

Divide the batter between the prepared pans and smooth level. Bake in the preheated oven for 25 minutes, or until golden and firm to the touch. Let cool in the pans for 5 minutes, then turn out and cool completely on a wire rack.

Sift the confectioners' sugar into a bowl and add the remaining butter and coconut cream. Beat together until smooth. Spread the pineapple jelly over one of the cakes and top with just under half of the buttercream. Place the second cake on top. Spread the remaining buttercream on top of the cake and scatter with the toasted coconut.

Red Velvet Cake

Serves 12

1 cup unsalted butter,
 plus extra for greasing

4 tbsp water

$\frac{1}{2}$ cup unsweetened cocoa

3 eggs

generous 1 cup buttermilk

2 tsp vanilla extract

2 tbsp red food coloring

$2\frac{1}{2}$ cups all-purpose flour

$\frac{1}{2}$ cup cornstarch

$1\frac{1}{2}$ tsp baking powder

scant $1\frac{1}{2}$ cups superfine sugar

Frosting

generous 1 cup cream cheese

3 tbsp unsalted butter

3 tbsp superfine sugar

1 tsp vanilla extract

Preheat the oven to 375°F/190°C. Grease and line the bottoms of two 9-inch/23-cm round layer cake pans.

Place the butter, water, and cocoa in a small saucepan and heat gently, without boiling, stirring until melted and smooth. Remove from the heat and let cool slightly.

Beat together the eggs, buttermilk, vanilla extract, and food coloring until frothy. Beat in the butter mixture. Sift together the flour, cornstarch, and baking powder, then stir into the mixture with the sugar.

Divide the batter between the prepared pans and bake in the preheated oven for 25–30 minutes, or until risen and firm to the touch. Cool in the pans for 3–4 minutes, then turn out and cool completely on a wire rack.

For the frosting, beat together all the ingredients until smooth. Use about half of the frosting to sandwich the cakes together, then spread the remainder over the top, swirling with a metal spatula.

Date & Walnut Loaf

Serves 8

generous ½ cup chopped
    pitted dates

½ tsp baking soda

finely grated rind of ½ lemon

scant ½ cup hot tea

3 tbsp unsalted butter, plus extra
    for greasing

⅓ cup light brown sugar

1 medium egg

generous 1 cup self-rising flour

¼ cup chopped walnuts

walnut halves, to decorate

Preheat the oven to 350°F/180°C. Grease and line an 8 x 4 x 2-inch/20 x 10 x 5-cm loaf pan.

Place the dates, baking soda, and lemon rind in a bowl and add the hot tea. Let soak for 10 minutes, until softened.

Cream together the butter and sugar until light and fluffy, then beat in the egg. Stir in the date mixture.

Fold in the flour using a large metal spoon, then fold in the chopped walnuts. Spoon the mixture into the prepared pan and smooth level. Top with the walnut halves.

Bake in the preheated oven for 35–40 minutes, or until risen, firm, and golden brown. Cool for 10 minutes in the pan, then turn out and cool completely on a wire rack.

great tip!
to serve, cut the loaf into
slices and butter thickly

Sticky Ginger Loaf

Serves 8–10

butter, for greasing

1½ cups all-purpose flour

1 tbsp baking powder

1 tbsp ground ginger

¾ cup sunflower oil

scant ½ cup dark brown sugar

⅓ cup dark corn syrup

3 eggs, beaten

3 pieces preserved ginger in syrup,
  drained and finely chopped,
  plus 2 tbsp syrup from the jar

sliced preserved ginger, to decorate

Preheat the oven to 350°F/180°C. Grease and line a 5-cup loaf pan.

Sift the flour, baking powder, and ground ginger into a large bowl. Add the oil, sugar, corn syrup, and eggs, then beat well to a smooth batter. Stir in the chopped ginger.

Pour the batter into the prepared pan. Bake in the preheated oven for 1–1¼ hours, or until well risen and firm to the touch.

Let cool in the pan for 10 minutes, then turn out and finish cooling on a wire rack. To serve, brush the cake with the ginger syrup, arrange the sliced ginger on top, and cut into slices.

great tip!
this will taste even better if kept in an airtight container for a day before eating

Apple Pie

Serves 6

Pie dough

2½ cups all-purpose flour

pinch of salt

6 tbsp cold unsalted butter or
   margarine, cut into
   small pieces

6 tbsp cold lard or vegetable
   shortening, cut into
   small pieces

1–2 tbsp cold water

beaten egg or milk, for glazing

Filling

1 lb 10 oz–2 lb 4 oz/750 g–1 kg
   baking apples, peeled, cored,
   and sliced

scant ⅔ cup brown or superfine
   sugar, plus extra for sprinkling

½–1 tsp ground cinnamon,
   allspice, or ground ginger

1–2 tbsp water (optional)

To make the pie dough, sift the flour and salt into a large bowl. Rub in the butter and lard until the mixture resembles breadcrumbs. Add the water and mix to a dough. Wrap in plastic wrap and chill for 30 minutes.

Preheat the oven to 425°F/220°C. Roll out almost two-thirds of the pie dough thinly and use to line a deep 9-inch/23-cm pie plate or pie pan.

Mix the apples with the sugar and spice and pack into the pastry shell. Add the water if needed, particularly if the apples are not very juicy.

Roll out the remaining pie dough to form a lid. Dampen the edges of the pie rim with water and position the lid, pressing the edges firmly together. Trim and crimp the edges.

Use the trimmings to cut out leaves or other shapes to decorate the top of the pie. Dampen and attach. Glaze the top of the pie with beaten egg or milk, make one or two slits in the top, and place the pie on a baking sheet.

Bake in the preheated oven for 20 minutes, then reduce the oven temperature to 350°F/180°C and bake for an additional 30 minutes, or until golden brown. Serve hot or cold, sprinkled with sugar.

Latticed Cherry Pie

Serves 8

Pie dough

1 cup all-purpose flour,
   plus extra for dusting

¼ tsp baking powder

½ tsp ground allspice

½ tsp salt

¼ cup superfine sugar

4 tbsp cold unsalted butter,
   diced, plus extra for greasing

1 egg, beaten, plus extra
   for glazing

Filling

6 cups pitted fresh cherries or
   drained canned cherries

½ cup superfine sugar

½ tsp almond extract

2 tsp cherry brandy

¼ tsp ground allspice

2 tbsp cornstarch

2 tbsp water

2 tbsp unsalted butter, diced

To make the pie dough, sift the flour, baking powder, allspice, and salt into a large bowl. Stir in the sugar. Rub in the butter until the mixture resembles breadcrumbs. Add the egg and mix to a dough. Wrap in plastic wrap and chill for 30 minutes.

Preheat the oven to 425°F/220°C. Grease a 9-inch/23-cm tart pan. Roll out the pie dough into two 12-inch/30-cm circles and use one to line the prepared pan.

Put half the cherries and the sugar into a saucepan. Simmer over low heat, stirring, for 5 minutes, or until the sugar has melted. Stir in the almond extract, brandy, and allspice. Mix together the cornstarch and water. Remove the pan from the heat and stir in the cornstarch paste, then return to the heat and stir constantly until the mixture boils and thickens. Let cool slightly. Stir in the remaining cherries, pour into the pastry shell, and dot with the butter.

Cut the second dough circle into 11 strips and place over the filling to form a lattice. Trim off the edges, crimp the rim, and brush with beaten egg. Cover with foil, then bake in the preheated oven for 30 minutes. Discard the foil, then bake for an additional 15 minutes, or until golden.

Key Lime Pie

Serves 6–8

Crumb crust

6 oz/175 g graham crackers or
  gingersnaps

2 tbsp superfine sugar

½ tsp ground cinnamon

6 tbsp unsalted butter, melted,
  plus extra for greasing

Filling

14 oz/400g canned condensed
  milk

½ cup lime juice

finely grated rind of 3 limes

4 extra large egg yolks

Preheat the oven to 325°F/160°C. Lightly grease a 9-inch/23-cm pie plate that is about 1½ inches/4 cm deep.

To make the crumb crust, put the crackers, sugar, and cinnamon into a food processor and process until fine crumbs form—do not overprocess to a powder. Add the melted butter and process again until moistened.

Turn the crumb mixture into the prepared pie plate and press over the bottom and up the sides. Transfer to a baking sheet and bake in the preheated oven for 5 minutes.

Meanwhile, beat the condensed milk, lime juice, lime rind, reserving some for decoration, and egg yolks together in a bowl until well blended.

Remove the crumb crust from the oven, pour in the filling, and spread out to the edges. Bake for an additional 15 minutes, or until the filling is set around the edges but still wobbly in the center. Remove from the oven and let cool completely, then cover and chill in the refrigerator for at least 2 hours. Decorate with the reserved lime rind before serving.

Boston Cream Pie

Serves 6–8

1 package (1 lb 3 oz/525 g)
   white or yellow cake mix

Pastry cream

½ cup superfine sugar

2 tbsp cornstarch

3 eggs

1 cup whipping cream

1 cup milk

1 tbsp unsalted butter

1½ tsp vanilla extract

pinch of salt

Chocolate topping

4 oz/115 g semisweet chocolate,
   chopped

½ cup heavy cream

1 tsp unsalted butter

For the pastry cream, beat together the sugar, cornstarch, and eggs until the beater leaves a ribbon trail when lifted. Set aside. Bring the cream, milk, and butter to a boil in a saucepan. Add the sugar mixture and boil, beating constantly, for 1 minute, until thickened, then strain into a bowl. Cover the surface with plastic wrap and chill overnight.

For the chocolate topping, put the chocolate into a heatproof bowl. Bring the cream and butter to simmering point in a small saucepan, then pour over the chocolate. Let stand for 3 minutes, then whisk gently to mix. Let cool and thicken.

Make up the cake mix according to the package directions using two round layer cake pans. Turn out the cakes onto wire racks and cool completely before assembling.

Whisk the vanilla extract and salt into the pastry cream, then spread it over one of the cakes. Top with the second cake, then spread the chocolate topping evenly over the top. Chill in the refrigerator until the chocolate has firmed up before serving.

New York Cheesecake

Serves 10

5½ oz/150 g graham crackers

1 tbsp granulated sugar

generous ½ cup unsalted butter,
   melted, plus extra for greasing

2 lb/900 g cream cheese

1¼ cups superfine sugar

2 tbsp all-purpose flour

1 tsp vanilla extract

finely grated rind of 1 orange

finely grated rind of 1 lemon

3 eggs

2 egg yolks

1¼ cups heavy cream

Preheat the oven to 350°F/180°C. Grease a 9-inch/23-cm round, springform cake pan.

To make the crumb crust, put the crackers and granulated sugar into food processor and process until fine crumbs form—do not overprocess to a powder. Add the melted butter and process again until moistened. Turn the crumb mixture into the prepared pan and press over the bottom. Bake in the preheated oven for 10 minutes. Let cool on a wire rack.

Increase the oven temperature to 400°F/200°C. Using an electric mixer, beat the cream cheese, then gradually add the superfine sugar and flour and beat until smooth. Increase the speed and beat in the vanilla extract, orange rind, and lemon rind, then add in the eggs and egg yolks, one at a time. Finally, beat in the cream. The mixture should be light and fluffy.

Pour the cream cheese mixture into the pan and smooth level. Transfer to the oven and bake for 15 minutes, then reduce the temperature to 200°F/100°C and bake for an additional 30 minutes. Turn off the oven and let the cheesecake stand for 2 hours to cool and set. Cover and chill overnight.

Mississippi Mud Pie

Serves 12–14

Crumb crust

5 oz/140 g graham crackers

½ cup finely chopped pecans

1 tbsp light brown sugar

½ tsp ground cinnamon

6 tbsp unsalted butter, melted

Filling

1 cup unsalted butter or margarine, plus extra for greasing

6 oz/175 g semisweet chocolate, chopped

½ cup dark corn syrup

4 extra large eggs, beaten

½ cup finely chopped pecans

Preheat the oven to 350°F/180°C. Lightly grease a 9-inch/23-cm round, springform cake pan.

To make the crumb crust, put the crackers, pecans, sugar, and cinnamon into a food processor and process until fine crumbs form—do not overprocess to a powder. Add the melted butter and process again until moistened.

Put the crumb mixture into the prepared pan and press over the bottom and about 1½ inches/4 cm up the sides of the pan. Cover the pan and let chill while you make the filling.

To make the filling, put the butter, chocolate, and corn syrup into a pan over low heat and stir until melted and blended. Let cool, then beat in the eggs and pecans.

Pour the filling into the pan and smooth level. Bake in the preheated oven for 30 minutes, or until just set but still soft in the center. Let cool on a wire rack. Serve at room temperature or chilled.

Sweet Pumpkin Pie

Serves 6–8

4 lb/1.8 kg sweet pumpkin,
   halved and seeded

1 cup all-purpose flour,
   plus extra for dusting

¼ tsp baking powder

1½ tsp ground cinnamon

¾ tsp ground nutmeg

¾ tsp ground cloves

1 tsp salt

¼ cup superfine sugar

4 tbsp cold unsalted butter,
   diced, plus extra for greasing

3 eggs

14 oz/400 g canned condensed
   milk

½ tsp vanilla extract

1 tbsp raw brown sugar

Streusel topping

2 tbsp all-purpose flour

4 tbsp raw brown sugar

1 tsp ground cinnamon

2 tbsp cold unsalted butter, diced

generous ⅔ cup chopped pecans

generous ⅔ cup chopped walnuts

Preheat the oven to 375°F/190°C. Put the pumpkin halves, face down, in a baking pan and cover with foil. Bake in the preheated oven for 1½ hours. Scoop out the flesh and puree in a food processor. Drain off any excess liquid.

Grease a 9-inch/23-cm round tart pan. Sift the flour and baking powder into a bowl. Stir in ½ teaspoon of the cinnamon, ¼ teaspoon of the nutmeg, ¼ teaspoon of the cloves, ½ teaspoon of the salt, and the superfine sugar. Rub in the butter until the mixture resembles breadcrumbs. Lightly beat one of the eggs, then add to the bowl. Mix together to form a dough, then roll out on a lightly floured surface and use to line the prepared pan. Chill for 30 minutes.

Preheat the oven to 425°F/220°C. Put the pumpkin in a bowl, then stir in the condensed milk and the remaining eggs. Add the remaining spices and salt, then stir in the vanilla extract and raw brown sugar. Pour into the pastry shell and bake in the preheated oven for 15 minutes.

Mix the flour, raw brown sugar, and cinnamon in a bowl. Rub in the butter, then stir in the nuts. Remove the pie from the oven and reduce the heat to 350°F/180°C. Sprinkle over the topping, then bake for an additional 35 minutes. Serve hot or cold.

Sweet Potato Pie

Serves 8

Pie dough

1¼ cups all-purpose flour, plus extra for dusting

½ tsp salt

¼ tsp superfine sugar

1½ tbsp cold unsalted butter, diced

3 tbsp cold shortening, diced

2 tbsp cold water

Filling

1 lb 2 oz/500 g orange-flesh sweet potatoes, peeled

3 extra large eggs, beaten

½ cup light brown sugar

12 oz/350 g canned condensed milk

3 tbsp unsalted butter, melted

2 tsp vanilla extract

1 tsp ground cinnamon

1 tsp ground nutmeg

½ tsp salt

Sift the flour, salt, and superfine sugar into a bowl. Add the butter and shortening and rub in until the mixture resembles fine breadcrumbs. Add the water and mix to a dough. Wrap in plastic wrap and chill for at least 1 hour.

Cook the sweet potatoes in a saucepan of boiling water for 15 minutes. Drain. When cool, mash the potatoes in a bowl and beat in the eggs and brown sugar until very smooth. Beat in the remaining filling ingredients and set aside.

Preheat the oven to 425°F/220°C. Roll out the pie dough on a lightly floured surface into a thin 11-inch/28-cm circle and use to line a 9-inch/23-cm tart pan that is about 1½ inches/4 cm deep. Press a floured fork around the edges and prick the bottom all over. Line with parchment paper, fill with dried beans, and bake in the preheated oven for 12 minutes, until light golden. Remove the paper and beans.

Pour the filling into the pastry shell and bake for 10 minutes. Reduce the oven temperature to 325°F/160°C and bake for an additional 35 minutes, or until a knife inserted into the center comes out clean. Let cool on a wire rack.

Rhubarb Crumble

Serves 6

2 lb/900 g rhubarb

½ cup superfine sugar

juice and grated rind of 1 orange

cream, to serve

Crumble topping

generous 1½ cups all-purpose
  flour

½ cup cold unsalted butter, diced

½ cup light brown sugar

1 tsp ground ginger

Preheat the oven to 375°F/190°C. Cut the rhubarb into 1-inch/2.5-cm lengths and put in an baking dish with the superfine sugar and the orange juice and rind.

To make the crumble topping, sift the flour into a bowl. Rub in the butter with your fingertips until the mixture resembles fine breadcrumbs. Stir in the brown sugar and ginger. Spread evenly over the fruit and press down lightly with a fork.

Place the dish on a baking sheet and bake in the center of the preheated oven for 25–30 minutes, until the crumble is golden brown. Serve warm with cream.

variation
for a change, add oats or nuts to the crumble topping

Bread & Butter Pudding

Serves 4–6

5 tbsp unsalted butter, softened,
    plus extra for greasing

6 slices of thick white bread

⅓ cup mixed dried fruit

1 tbsp chopped candied peel

3 extra large eggs

1¼ cups milk

⅔ cup heavy cream

¼ cup superfine sugar

1 tbsp raw brown sugar

freshly grated nutmeg, to taste

Preheat the oven to 350°F/180°C. Grease an 8 x 10-inch/20 x 25-cm baking dish. Spread the butter over the slices of bread. Cut each slice of bread diagonally into quarters, then arrange half the bread overlapping in the prepared baking dish.

Scatter half the mixed dried fruit and peel over the bread, cover with the remaining bread, and add the remaining fruit and peel.

In a pitcher, beat the eggs well and stir in the milk, cream, and superfine sugar. Pour into the baking dish and let stand for 15 minutes to let the bread soak up some of the egg mixture.

Tuck the dried fruit and peel under the bread slices so that they don't burn. Sprinkle over the raw brown sugar and nutmeg to taste.

Place the dish on a baking sheet and bake at the top of the preheated oven for 30–40 minutes, until just set and golden brown. Serve warm.

Cupcakes & Muffins

Vanilla Frosted Cupcakes

Makes 12

½ cup unsalted butter, softened

generous ½ cup superfine sugar

2 eggs, lightly beaten

1 cup self-rising flour

1 tbsp milk

1 tbsp colored sprinkles

Frosting

¾ cup unsalted butter, softened

1 tsp vanilla extract

2½ cups confectioners' sugar

Preheat the oven to 350°F/180°C. Put 12 paper liners in a shallow muffin pan.

Cream together the butter and sugar until pale and fluffy. Gradually beat in the eggs. Sift in the flour and, using a metal spoon, fold in with the milk. Spoon the batter into the paper liners.

Bake in the preheated oven for 20 minutes, or until golden brown and firm to the touch. Transfer to a wire rack and let cool.

To make the frosting, put the butter and vanilla extract in a bowl and, using an electric mixer, beat until the butter is pale and very soft. Gradually sift in the confectioners' sugar, beating well after each addition.

Spoon the frosting into a large pastry bag fitted with a medium star tip and pipe a swirl of frosting on top of each cupcake. Decorate with the colored sprinkles.

Chocolate Hazelnut Cupcakes

Makes 18

¾ cup unsalted butter, softened

generous ½ cup light brown sugar

2 extra large eggs, lightly beaten

2 tbsp chocolate-and-hazelnut
   spread

1¼ cups self-rising flour

scant ½ cup blanched hazelnuts,
   coarsely ground

Topping

5 tbsp chocolate-and-hazelnut
   spread

18 whole blanched hazelnuts

Preheat the oven to 350°F/180°C. Put 18 paper liners in two shallow muffin pans.

Cream together the butter and sugar until pale and fluffy. Gradually beat in the eggs, then stir in the chocolate-and-hazelnut spread. Sift in the flour and, using a metal spoon, fold in with the ground hazelnuts. Spoon the batter into the paper liners.

Bake in the preheated oven for 20–25 minutes, or until risen and firm to the touch. Transfer to a wire rack and let cool.

When the cupcakes are cold, swirl a little of the chocolate-and-hazelnut spread over the top of each cupcake and top with a hazelnut.

great tip!
make a hollow in the top
of the cooked cupcakes and
fill with chocolate-and-
hazelnut spread

Blueberry Cupcakes with Sour Cream Frosting

Makes 30

1½ cups all-purpose flour

1 tbsp baking powder

¾ cup unsalted butter, softened

generous ¾ cup superfine sugar

3 eggs, beaten

1 tsp vanilla extract

finely grated rind of ½ orange

1⅓ cups fresh blueberries

Frosting

3 tbsp sour cream

1⅓ cups confectioners' sugar

Preheat the oven to 375°F/190°C. Put 30 paper liners into shallow muffin pans.

Sift the flour and baking powder into a large bowl and add the butter, superfine sugar, eggs, and vanilla extract. Beat well until smooth, then stir in the orange rind and scant 1 cup of the blueberries. Spoon the batter into the paper liners.

Bake in the preheated oven for 15–20 minutes, or until risen, firm, and golden brown. Transfer to a wire rack and let cool.

For the frosting, stir the sour cream into the confectioners' sugar and mix well until smooth. Spoon a little on top of each cupcake and top with the remaining blueberries. Let set.

variation
top the cupcakes with melted
white chocolate instead

Gooey Chocolate & Cream Cheese Cupcakes

Makes 12

1¼ cups all-purpose flour

¼ cup unsweetened cocoa

¾ tsp baking soda

1 cup superfine sugar

¼ cup sunflower oil

¾ cup water

2 tsp white vinegar

½ tsp vanilla extract

⅔ cup cream cheese

1 egg, lightly beaten

generous ½ cup semisweet
   chocolate chips

Preheat the oven to 350°F/180°C. Put 12 paper liners in a muffin pan.

Sift the flour, cocoa, and baking soda into a large bowl. Stir in ¾ cup of the sugar. Add the oil, water, vinegar, and vanilla extract, then stir well together until combined.

Place the remaining sugar, the cream cheese, and egg in a large bowl and beat together until well mixed. Stir in the chocolate chips.

Spoon the batter into the paper liners and top each with a spoonful of the cream cheese mixture.

Bake in the preheated oven for 25 minutes, or until firm to the touch. Let the cupcakes cool in the pan for 10 minutes, then transfer to a wire rack to cool completely.

great tip!
for extra indulgence, serve these cupcakes with cream

Chocolate &
Orange Cupcakes

Makes 16

½ cup unsalted butter, softened

generous ½ cup superfine sugar

finely grated rind and juice
  of ½ orange

2 eggs, lightly beaten

generous ¾ cup self-rising flour

1 oz/25 g semisweet chocolate,
  grated

thin strips of candied orange peel,
  to decorate

Frosting

4 oz/115 g semisweet chocolate,
  broken into pieces

2 tbsp unsalted butter

1 tbsp light corn syrup

Preheat the oven to 350°F/180°C. Put 16 paper liners in shallow muffin pans.

Cream together the butter, sugar, and orange rind until pale and fluffy. Gradually beat in the eggs. Sift in the flour and, using a metal spoon, fold gently in with the orange juice and grated chocolate. Spoon the batter into the paper liners.

Bake in the preheated oven for 20 minutes, or until risen and golden brown. Transfer to a wire rack and let cool.

To make the frosting, put the chocolate into a heatproof bowl and add the butter and corn syrup. Set the bowl over a saucepan of simmering water and heat until melted. Remove from the heat and stir until smooth. Let cool until the frosting is thick enough to spread. Spread over the cupcakes and decorate each cupcake with a few strips of candied orange peel. Let set.

Maple Pecan Cupcakes

Makes 30

1½ cups all-purpose flour

1 tbsp baking powder

¾ cup unsalted butter, softened

generous ½ cup light brown sugar

4 tbsp maple syrup

3 eggs, beaten

1 tsp vanilla extract

¼ cups finely chopped pecans

Topping

⅓ cup finely chopped pecans

2 tbsp all-purpose flour

2 tbsp light brown sugar

2 tbsp melted unsalted butter

Preheat the oven to 375°F/190°C. Put 30 paper liners into shallow muffin pans.

Sift the flour and baking powder into a large bowl and add the butter, sugar, maple syrup, eggs, and vanilla extract. Beat well until the mixture is smooth, then stir in the pecans. Spoon the batter into the paper liners.

For the topping, combine the pecans, flour, sugar, and melted butter to make a crumbly mixture and spoon a little on top of each cake.

Bake in the preheated oven for 15–20 minutes, or until risen, firm, and golden brown. Transfer to a wire rack and let cool.

great tip!
brush the tops of the cupcakes with maple syrup to glaze

Black Forest Cupcakes

Makes 12

3 oz/75 g semisweet chocolate,
  broken into pieces

1 tsp lemon juice

4 tbsp milk

generous 1 cup self-rising flour

1 tbsp unsweetened cocoa,
  plus extra for dusting

½ tsp baking soda

2 eggs

4 tbsp butter, softened

generous ½ cup light brown sugar

generous 2 tbsp chopped dried
  sweetened sour cherries

2 tbsp cherry liqueur (optional)

⅔ cup heavy cream

5 tbsp cherry conserve

Preheat the oven to 350°F/180°C. Put 12 paper liners in a muffin pan.

Put the chocolate into a heatproof bowl and set the bowl over a saucepan of gently simmering water until melted. Remove from the heat and let cool slightly. Add the lemon juice to the milk and let stand for 10 minutes—it will curdle a little.

Sift the flour, cocoa powder, and baking soda into a bowl. Add the eggs, butter, sugar, and the milk mixture and beat with an electric mixer until smooth. Fold in the melted chocolate and the sour cherries. Spoon the batter into the paper liners.

Bake in the preheated oven for 20–25 minutes, until risen and firm to the touch. Transfer to a wire rack and let cool.

When cold, use a serrated knife to cut a circle from the top of each cupcake. Sprinkle the cakes with a little cherry liqueur, if using. Beat the cream until it holds soft peaks, then spoon into the centers of the cupcakes and top with a small spoonful of conserve. Gently replace the cupcake tops and dust lightly with cocoa. Chill in the refrigerator until ready to serve.

Carrot Cake Cupcakes

Make 12

¾ cup unsalted butter, softened

generous ½ cup superfine sugar

2 eggs, lightly beaten

generous 1½ cups grated carrot

½ cup finely chopped walnuts

2 tbsp orange juice

grated rind of ½ orange

1¼ cups self-rising flour

1 tsp ground cinnamon

walnut halves, to decorate

Frosting

½ cup cream cheese

2 cups confectioners' sugar

1 tbsp orange juice

Preheat the oven to 350°F/180°C. Put 12 paper liners in a shallow muffin pan.

Cream together the butter and superfine sugar until pale and fluffy. Gradually beat in the eggs. Fold in the grated carrot, chopped walnuts, and the orange juice and rind. Sift in the flour and cinnamon and, using a metal spoon, fold in until just combined. Spoon the batter into the paper liners.

Bake in the preheated oven for 15–20 minutes, or until golden brown and firm to the touch. Transfer to a wire rack and let cool.

To make the frosting, place the cream cheese, confectioners' sugar, and orange juice in a bowl and beat together. Spread over the top of the cupcakes, then decorate with walnut halves.

great tip!
top the cupcakes with little carrot decorations, available from grocery stores

Spiced Apple Pie Cupcakes

Make 12

3½ tbsp unsalted butter, softened

⅓ cup raw brown sugar

1 egg, lightly beaten

generous 1 cup all-purpose flour

1½ tsp baking powder

½ tsp apple pie spice

1 large baking apple, peeled, cored,
   and finely chopped

1 tbsp orange juice

Topping

5 tbsp all-purpose flour

½ tsp apple pie spice

¼ cup superfine sugar

2 tbsp unsalted butter

Preheat the oven to 350°F/180°C. Put 12 paper liners in a muffin pan.

To make the topping, place the flour, apple pie spice, and superfine sugar in a large bowl. Add the butter and rub in with your fingertips until the mixture resembles fine breadcrumbs. Set aside.

Cream together the butter and raw brown sugar until pale and fluffy. Gradually beat in the egg. Sift in the flour, baking powder, and apple pie spice and fold in, then stir in the chopped apple and orange juice. Spoon the batter into the paper liners. Sprinkle the topping over the cupcakes and press down gently.

Bake in the preheated oven for 30 minutes, or until golden brown. Transfer to a wire rack and let cool.

Low-Fat Blueberry Muffins

Makes 12

oil or melted butter,
   for greasing (if using)

generous 1½ cups all-purpose flour

1 tsp baking soda

¼ tsp salt

1 tsp allspice

generous ½ cup superfine sugar

3 extra large egg whites

3 tbsp low-fat margarine

⅔ cup thick low-fat plain yogurt or
   blueberry-flavored yogurt

1 tsp vanilla extract

¾ cup fresh blueberries

Preheat the oven to 375°F/190°C. Put 12 paper liners in a muffin pan or brush the cups with oil or melted butter.

Sift the flour, baking soda, salt, and half the allspice into a large mixing bowl. Add 6 tablespoons of the superfine sugar and mix together.

In a separate bowl, beat the egg whites. Add the margarine, yogurt, and vanilla extract and mix together well, then stir in the blueberries until thoroughly incorporated. Add to the flour ingredients. Stir gently until just combined; do not overmix.

Spoon the batter into the prepared muffin pan. Mix the remaining sugar with the remaining allspice, then sprinkle over the tops of the muffins.

Bake in the preheated oven for 25 minutes, or until risen and golden. Let the muffins cool in the pan for 5 minutes, then serve warm or transfer to a wire rack and let cool completely.

Mint Chocolate Chip Muffins

Makes 12

oil or melted butter,
   for greasing (if using)

2 cups all-purpose flour

1 tbsp baking powder

pinch of salt

generous ½ cup superfine sugar

1 cup semisweet chocolate chips

2 eggs

1 cup milk

6 tbsp sunflower oil or melted,
   cooled unsalted butter

1 tsp peppermint extract

a few drops of green food coloring
   (optional)

confectioners' sugar,
   for dusting

Preheat the oven to 400°F/200°C. Put 12 paper liners in a muffin pan or brush the cups with oil or melted butter.

Sift together the flour, baking powder, and salt into a large bowl. Stir in the superfine sugar and chocolate chips.

Lightly beat the eggs in a large pitcher or bowl, then beat in the milk, oil, and peppermint extract. Add the food coloring, if using, to color the mixture a very subtle shade of green. Make a well in the center of the dry ingredients and pour in the beaten liquid ingredients. Stir gently until just combined; do not overmix.

Spoon the batter into the prepared muffin pan. Bake in the preheated oven for about 20 minutes, until well risen and firm to the touch.

Let the muffins cool in the pan for 5 minutes, then serve warm or transfer to a wire rack and let cool completely. Dust with confectioners' sugar before serving.

Dark Chocolate & Ginger Muffins

Makes 12

oil or melted butter,
    for greasing (if using)

generous 1½ cups all-purpose
    flour

½ cup unsweetened cocoa

1 tbsp baking powder

1 tbsp ground ginger

pinch of salt

generous ½ cup dark brown
    sugar

3 pieces preserved ginger in
    syrup, drained and finely
    chopped, plus 2 tbsp syrup
    from the jar

2 eggs

1 cup milk

6 tbsp sunflower oil or melted,
    cooled unsalted butter

Preheat the oven to 400°F/200°C. Put 12 paper liners in a muffin pan or brush the cups with oil or melted butter.

Sift together the flour, cocoa, baking powder, ground ginger, and salt into a large bowl. Stir in the sugar and preserved ginger.

Lightly beat the eggs in a large pitcher or bowl, then beat in the milk, oil, and ginger syrup. Make a well in the center of the dry ingredients and pour in the beaten liquid ingredients. Stir gently until just combined; do not overmix.

Spoon the batter into the prepared muffin pan. Bake in the preheated oven for about 20 minutes, until well risen and firm to the touch.

Let the muffins cool in the pan for 5 minutes, then serve warm or transfer to a wire rack and let cool completely.

Rocky Road Chocolate Muffins

Makes 12

oil or melted butter, for greasing
   (if using)

generous 1½ cups all-purpose flour

½ cup unsweetened cocoa

1 tbsp baking powder

pinch of salt

generous ½ cup superfine sugar

generous ½ cup white
   chocolate chips

½ cup white miniature
   marshmallows, cut in half

2 eggs

1 cup milk

6 tbsp sunflower oil or melted,
   cooled unsalted butter

Preheat the oven to 400°F/200°C. Put 12 paper liners in a muffin pan or brush the cups with oil or melted butter.

Sift together the flour, cocoa, baking powder, and salt into a large bowl. Stir in the sugar, chocolate chips, and marshmallows.

Lightly beat the eggs in a large pitcher or bowl, then beat in the milk and oil. Make a well in the center of the dry ingredients and pour in the beaten liquid ingredients. Stir gently until just combined; do not overmix.

Spoon the batter into the prepared muffin pan. Bake in the preheated oven for about 20 minutes, until risen and firm to the touch.

Let the muffins cool in the pan for 5 minutes, then serve warm or transfer to a wire rack and let cool completely.

variation
use ⅓ cup white chocolate chips and add generous ½ cup chopped Brazil nuts

Lemon & Poppy Seed Muffins

Makes 12

oil or melted butter, for greasing
    (if using)
2 cups all-purpose flour
1 tbsp baking powder
pinch of salt
generous ½ cup superfine sugar
2 tbsp poppy seeds
2 eggs
1 cup milk
6 tbsp sunflower oil or melted,
    cooled unsalted butter
finely grated rind of 2 lemons

Preheat the oven to 400°F/200°C. Put 12 paper liners in a muffin pan or brush the cups with oil or melted butter.

Sift together the flour, baking powder, and salt into a large bowl. Stir in the sugar and poppy seeds.

Lightly beat the eggs in a large pitcher or bowl, then beat in the milk, oil, and lemon rind. Make a well in the center of the dry ingredients and pour in the beaten liquid ingredients. Stir gently until just combined; do not overmix.

Spoon the batter into the prepared muffin pan. Bake in the preheated oven for about 20 minutes, until well risen, golden brown, and firm to the touch.

Let the muffins cool in the pan for 5 minutes, then serve warm or transfer to a wire rack and let cool completely.

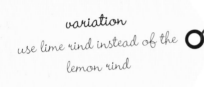

variation
use lime rind instead of the lemon rind

Toasted Almond & Apricot Muffins

Makes 12

generous ½ cup dried apricots

3 tbsp orange juice

⅓ cup blanched almonds

oil or melted butter,
    for greasing (if using)

2 cups all-purpose flour

1 tbsp baking powder

pinch of salt

generous ½ cup superfine sugar

2 eggs

scant 1 cup buttermilk

6 tbsp sunflower oil or melted,
    cooled unsalted butter

¼ tsp almond extract

generous ⅓ cup slivered almonds

Cut the apricots into small pieces and put in a bowl. Add the orange juice and let soak for 1 hour.

Meanwhile, toast the blanched almonds under a preheated broiler, turning frequently, until golden. When cool, coarsely chop the almonds.

Preheat the oven to 400°F/200°C. Put 12 paper liners in a muffin pan or brush the cups with oil or melted butter. Sift together the flour, baking powder, and salt into a large bowl. Stir in the sugar and chopped almonds.

Lightly beat the eggs in a large pitcher or bowl, then beat in the buttermilk, oil, and almond extract. Make a well in the center of the dry ingredients, pour in the beaten liquid ingredients, and add the soaked apricots. Stir gently until just combined; do not overmix.

Spoon the batter into the prepared muffin pan. Sprinkle the slivered almonds over the tops of the muffins. Bake in the preheated oven for about 20 minutes, until well risen, golden brown, and firm to the touch.

Let the muffins cool in the pan for 5 minutes, then serve warm or transfer to a wire rack and let cool competely.

Crunchy Peanut Butter Muffins

Makes 12

oil or melted butter, for greasing
   (if using)

2 cups all-purpose flour

1 tbsp baking powder

pinch of salt

generous ½ cup dark brown sugar

2 eggs

¾ cup milk

6 tbsp sunflower oil or melted,
   cooled unsalted butter

generous ½ cup chunky peanut
   butter

Peanut topping

⅓ cup unsalted roasted peanuts

3 tbsp raw brown sugar

Preheat the oven to 400°F/200°C. Put 12 paper liners in a muffin pan or brush the cups with oil or melted butter.

To make the peanut topping, finely chop the peanuts. Put in a bowl, add the raw brown sugar, and mix together. Set aside.

Sift together the flour, baking powder, and salt into a large bowl. Stir in the dark brown sugar.

Lightly beat the eggs in a large pitcher or bowl, then beat in the milk, oil, and peanut butter. Make a well in the center of the dry ingredients and pour in the beaten liquid ingredients. Stir gently until just combined; do not overmix.

Spoon the batter into the prepared muffin pan. Sprinkle the peanut topping over the tops of the muffins. Bake in the preheated oven for about 20 minutes, until well risen, golden brown, and firm to the touch.

Let the muffins cool in the pan for 5 minutes, then serve warm or transfer to a wire rack and let cool completely.

Raspberry Crumble Muffins

Makes 12

oil or melted butter,
   for greasing (if using)

2 cups all-purpose flour

1 tbsp baking powder

½ tsp baking soda

pinch of salt

generous ½ cup superfine sugar

2 eggs

1 cup plain yogurt

6 tbsp sunflower oil or melted,
   cooled unsalted butter

1 tsp vanilla extract

scant 1 cup frozen raspberries

Crumble topping

½ cup all-purpose flour

3 tbsp unsalted butter, diced

2 tbsp superfine sugar

Preheat the oven to 400°F/200°C. Put 12 paper liners in a muffin pan or brush the cups with oil or melted butter.

To make the crumble topping, put the flour into a bowl. Add the butter and rub it in with your fingertips until the mixture resembles fine breadcrumbs. Stir in the sugar and set aside.

Sift together the flour, baking powder, baking soda, and salt into a large bowl. Stir in the sugar.

Lightly beat the eggs in a large pitcher or bowl, then beat in the yogurt, oil, and vanilla extract. Make a well in the center of the dry ingredients, pour in the beaten liquid ingredients, and add the raspberries. Stir gently until just combined; do not overmix.

Spoon the batter into the prepared muffin pan. Sprinkle the topping over the muffins and press down lightly. Bake in the preheated oven for about 20 minutes, until well risen, golden brown, and firm to the touch.

Let the muffins cool in the pan for 5 minutes, then serve warm or transfer to a wire rack and let cool completely.

Cranberry & Orange Muffins

Makes 12

scant 1½ cups dried cranberries

3 tbsp orange juice

oil or melted butter,
   for greasing (if using)

2 cups all-purpose flour

1 tbsp baking powder

pinch of salt

generous ½ cup superfine sugar

2 eggs

scant 1 cup milk

6 tbsp sunflower oil or melted,
   cooled unsalted butter

finely grated rind of 1 orange

Put the cranberries in a bowl, add the orange juice, and let soak for 1 hour.

Preheat the oven to 400°F/200°C. Put 12 paper liners in a muffin pan or brush the cups with oil or melted butter. Sift together the flour, baking powder, and salt into a large bowl. Stir in the sugar.

Lightly beat the eggs in a large pitcher or bowl, then beat in the milk, oil, and orange rind. Make a well in the center of the dry ingredients, pour in the beaten liquid ingredients, and add the soaked cranberries. Stir gently until just combined; do not overmix.

Spoon the batter into the prepared muffin pan. Bake in the preheated oven for about 20 minutes, until well risen, golden brown, and firm to the touch.

Let the muffins cool in the pan for 5 minutes, then serve warm or transfer to a wire rack and let cool completely.

Chile Cornbread Muffins

Makes 12

oil or melted butter,
   for greasing (if using)

1¼ cups all-purpose flour

4 tsp baking powder

1 tsp salt

1½ cups cornmeal

2 tbsp superfine sugar

4 scallions, finely chopped

1 fresh red chile, seeded and
   finely chopped

3 eggs

⅔ cup plain yogurt

⅔ cup milk

Preheat the oven to 400°F/200°C. Put 12 paper liners in a muffin pan or brush the cups with oil or melted butter. Sift together the flour, baking powder, and salt into a large bowl. Stir in the cornmeal, sugar, scallions, and chile.

Lightly beat the eggs in a large pitcher or bowl, then beat in the yogurt and milk. Make a well in the center of the dry ingredients and pour in the beaten liquid ingredients. Stir gently until just combined; do not overmix.

Spoon the batter into the prepared muffin pan. Bake in the preheated oven for 15–20 minutes, until well risen, golden brown, and firm to the touch.

Let the muffins cool in the pan for 5 minutes, then serve warm or transfer to a wire rack and let cool completely.

great tip!
dust the tops of the muffins with chili powder or paprika

Brownies & Bars

Chocolate Nut Brownies

Makes 16

8 oz/225 g semisweet chocolate,
  broken into pieces

¾ cup unsalted butter,
  plus extra for greasing

3 extra large eggs

½ cup superfine sugar

scant 1¼ cups self-rising flour

1 cup chopped walnuts or
  blanched hazelnuts

scant ⅓ cup milk chocolate chips

Preheat the oven to 350°F/180°C. Lightly grease a 10-inch/25-cm square, shallow cake pan.

Put the chocolate in a heatproof bowl and add the butter. Set the bowl over a saucepan of gently simmering water and heat until melted. Remove from the heat and stir until smooth. Let cool slightly.

Meanwhile, beat together the eggs and sugar in a bowl until pale and frothy. Stir in the chocolate mixture and then add the flour, walnuts, and chocolate chips. Mix together well.

Spoon the batter into the prepared pan. Bake in the preheated oven for 30 minutes, or until the top is set and the center is still slightly sticky. Let cool in the pan, then turn out and cut into squares.

great tip!
don't worry if the brownies sink or crack as they cool—this is normal

Chocolate Cheesecake Brownies

Makes 12

¾ cup unsalted butter,
  plus extra for greasing

3 tbsp unsweetened cocoa

1 cup superfine sugar

2 eggs, lightly beaten

1 cup all-purpose flour

Cheesecake swirl

generous 1 cup ricotta cheese

scant ¼ cup superfine sugar

1 egg

Preheat the oven to 350°F/180°C. Grease an 11 x 7-inch/28 x 18-cm baking pan.

Place the butter in a saucepan and heat gently until melted. Remove from the heat and stir in the cocoa and sugar. Beat in the eggs, add the flour, and stir to mix evenly. Spoon the batter into the prepared pan.

For the cheesecake swirl, place the ricotta, sugar, and egg in a bowl and beat together, then drop teaspoonfuls of the mixture over the chocolate mixture. Use a spatula to swirl the mixtures together lightly.

Bake in the preheated oven for 40–45 minutes, or until just firm to the touch. Let cool in the pan, then turn out and cut into bars.

variation
fold ¼ cup chocolate chips
  into the cheesecake swirl

Chocolate Fudge Brownies

Makes 16

scant 1 cup cream cheese

½ tsp vanilla extract

1 cup superfine sugar

2 eggs

6 tbsp unsalted butter,
  plus extra for greasing

3 tbsp unsweetened cocoa

¾ cup self-rising flour

⅓ cup chopped pecans

pecan halves, to decorate

Fudge frosting

4 tbsp unsalted butter

1 tbsp milk

⅔ cup confectioners' sugar

2 tbsp unsweetened cocoa

Preheat the oven to 350°F/180°C. Lightly grease and line an 8-inch/20-cm square, shallow cake pan.

Place the cream cheese, vanilla extract, and 5 teaspoons of the superfine sugar in a large bowl and beat together until smooth.

Place the eggs and the remaining sugar in a separate bowl and beat together until pale and frothy. Place the butter and cocoa in a small saucepan and heat gently, stirring, until the butter melts and the mixture combines. Remove from the heat, then stir into the egg mixture. Fold in the flour and chopped pecans.

Spoon half of the batter into the prepared pan and smooth level. Carefully spread the cream cheese mixture over the top, then cover with the remaining batter. Bake in the preheated oven for 40–45 minutes. Let cool in the pan.

To make the frosting, melt the butter in a saucepan with the milk. Stir in the confectioners' sugar and cocoa. Spread the frosting over the brownies and decorate with pecan halves. Let set, then cut into squares.

Cappuccino Brownies

Makes 15

1⅔ cups self-rising flour

1 tsp baking powder

1 tsp unsweetened cocoa,
   plus extra for dusting

1 cup unsalted butter, softened,
   plus extra for greasing

generous 1 cup superfine sugar

4 eggs, lightly beaten

3 tbsp instant coffee powder,
   dissolved in 2 tbsp hot water,
   cooled

White chocolate frosting

4 oz/115 g white chocolate,
   broken into pieces

4 tbsp unsalted butter, softened

3 tbsp milk

1½ cups confectioners' sugar

Preheat the oven to 350°F/180°C. Grease and line the bottom of an 11 x 7-inch/28 x 18-cm shallow baking pan.

Sift the flour, baking powder, and cocoa into a bowl and add the butter, superfine sugar, eggs, and coffee. Beat well until smooth, then spoon into the prepared pan and smooth level.

Bake in the preheated oven for 35–40 minutes, or until risen and firm to the touch. Cool in the pan for 10 minutes, then turn out and cool completely on a wire rack.

To make the frosting, place the chocolate, butter, and milk in a saucepan and heat gently, stirring, until the chocolate has melted. Remove the pan from the heat and sift in the confectioners' sugar. Beat until smooth, then spread over the top of the cake. Dust with cocoa and cut into squares.

Apple & Walnut Blondies

Makes 9

9 tbsp unsalted butter, softened,
   plus extra for greasing
1 cup light brown sugar
2 extra large eggs, lightly beaten
1 tsp vanilla extract
generous 1¾ cups all-purpose
   flour
1 tsp baking powder
1 small baking apple, peeled,
   cored, and finely chopped.
1 cup coarsely chopped walnuts
confectioners' sugar, for dusting

Preheat the oven to 350°F/180°C. Grease and line an 8-inch/20-cm square, shallow cake pan.

Cream together the butter and sugar until pale and fluffy. Gradually add the eggs and vanilla extract, beating well after each addition.

Sift in the flour and baking powder and fold in evenly. Add the apple and walnuts to the batter and stir together until well mixed.

Spoon the batter into the prepared pan and smooth level. Bake in the preheated oven for 40–45 minutes, or until risen and golden brown. Let cool in the pan, then dust with confectioners' sugar and cut into squares.

great tip!
don't chop the walnuts too
finely

Chocolate Chip & Ginger Blondies

Makes 9

generous ½ cup unsalted butter, softened, plus extra for greasing

1 cup light brown sugar

2 extra large eggs, lightly beaten

generous 1¾ cups all-purpose flour

1 tsp baking powder

1 tsp ground ginger

4 pieces preserved ginger in syrup, drained and finely chopped

generous ½ cup semisweet chocolate chips

confectioners' sugar, for dusting

Preheat the oven to 350°F/180°C. Grease and line an 8-inch/20-cm square, shallow cake pan.

Cream together the butter and brown sugar until pale and fluffy. Gradually add the eggs, beating well after each addition. Sift in the flour, baking powder, and ground ginger and beat together until mixed. Add the preserved ginger and chocolate chips and stir together until well mixed. Spoon the batter into the prepared pan and smooth level.

Bake in the preheated oven for 40–45 minutes, or until risen and golden brown. Let cool in the pan, then dust with confectioners' sugar and cut into squares.

variation
use white chocolate chips instead of semisweet chocolate chips

Banana & Carrot Squares

Makes 16

1½ cups all-purpose flour

1 tbsp baking powder

1 tsp ground nutmeg

¾ cup unsalted butter, softened, plus extra for greasing

generous ¾ cup superfine sugar

3 eggs, beaten

1 tbsp lemon juice

1 banana, mashed

1 cup grated carrots

⅓ cup finely chopped walnuts

dried banana chips and freshly grated nutmeg, to decorate

Frosting

generous 1 cup ricotta cheese

⅔ cup confectioners' sugar

finely grated rind of ½ lemon

Preheat the oven to 325°F/160°C. Grease and line a 9-inch/23-cm square cake pan.

Sift the flour, baking powder, and nutmeg into a bowl and add the butter, superfine sugar, and eggs. Beat well until smooth, then stir in the lemon juice, mashed banana, grated carrots, and walnuts.

Spoon the batter into the prepared pan and smooth level. Bake in the preheated oven for 45–55 minutes, or until well risen, firm, and golden brown.

Cool in the pan for 5 minutes, then turn out and cool completely on a wire rack. Cut into squares when cold.

For the frosting, combine the ricotta, confectioners' sugar, and lemon rind in a small bowl. Spoon or pipe a little frosting on top of each square of cake, top with a banana chip, and sprinkle with nutmeg.

Lemon Drizzle Bars

Makes 12

2 eggs

generous ¾ cup superfine sugar

⅔ cup soft margarine,
    plus extra for greasing

finely grated rind of 1 lemon

1½ cups self-rising flour

½ cup milk

confectioners' sugar, for dusting

Syrup

1¼ cups confectioners' sugar

¼ cup lemon juice

Preheat the oven to 350°F/180°C. Grease and line a 7-inch/18-cm square cake pan.

Place the eggs, superfine sugar, and margarine in a bowl and beat until smooth and fluffy. Stir in the lemon rind, then fold in the flour lightly and evenly. Stir in the milk, mixing evenly, then spoon the batter into the prepared cake pan and smooth level.

Bake in the preheated oven for 45–50 minutes, or until golden brown and firm to the touch. Remove from the oven and place the pan on a wire rack.

To make the syrup, place the confectioners' sugar and lemon juice in a small saucepan and heat gently, stirring until the sugar dissolves. Do not boil.

Prick the warm cake all over with a skewer and spoon the hot syrup evenly over the top.

Let cool completely in the pan, then turn out the cake, cut into bars, and dust with confectioners' sugar.

Coconut Bars

Makes 10

generous ½ cup unsalted butter, plus extra for greasing

generous 1 cup superfine sugar

2 eggs, lightly beaten

finely grated rind of 1 orange

3 tbsp orange juice

⅔ cup sour cream

1 cup self-rising flour

1 cup dry unsweetened coconut

toasted shredded coconut, to decorate

Frosting

1 egg white

1¾ cups confectioners' sugar

1 cup dry unsweetened coconut

about 1 tbsp orange juice

Preheat the oven to 350°F/180°C. Grease and line the bottom of a 9-inch/23-cm square cake pan.

Cream together the butter and superfine sugar until pale and fluffy. Gradually add the eggs, beating well after each addition. Stir in the orange rind, orange juice, and sour cream. Fold in the flour and dry unsweetened coconut evenly, then spoon the batter into the prepared pan and smooth level.

Bake in the preheated oven for 35–40 minutes, or until risen and firm to the touch. Cool in the pan for 10 minutes, then turn out and cool completely on a wire rack.

To make the frosting, place the egg white in a bowl and beat lightly, just enough to break it up. Stir in the confectioners' sugar and dry unsweetened coconut and add enough of the orange juice to mix to a thick paste. Spread over the top of the cake, sprinkle with toasted shredded coconut, then let set before slicing into bars.

Carrot Bars

Makes 14–16

¾ cup unsalted butter,
   plus extra for greasing
½ cup light brown sugar
2 eggs, beaten
scant ½ cup self-rising
   whole wheat flour
1 tsp baking powder
1 tsp ground cinnamon
generous 1 cup ground almonds
scant 1 cup grated carrot
½ cup golden raisins
½ cup finely chopped plumped
   dried apricots
scant ½ cup toasted chopped
   hazelnuts
1 tbsp slivered almonds

Preheat the oven to 350°F/180°C. Grease and line a 10 x 8-inch/25 x 20-cm shallow baking pan.

Cream together the butter and sugar until pale and fluffy. Gradually add the eggs, beating well after each addition.

Sift in the flour, baking powder, and cinnamon, adding any bran left in the sifter, and fold in lightly and evenly with a metal spoon. Fold in the ground almonds, grated carrot, golden raisins, apricots, and hazelnuts.

Spoon the batter into the prepared pan and sprinkle the slivered almonds over the top. Bake in the preheated oven for 35–45 minutes, or until a skewer inserted into the center comes out clean.

Remove from the oven and let cool in the pan, then turn out and cut into bars.

Coconut Paradise Bars

Makes 16

7 oz/200 g semisweet chocolate,
   broken into pieces

scant ½ cup unsalted butter, plus
   extra for greasing

1 cup superfine sugar

2 extra large eggs, lightly beaten

2¼ cups dry unsweetened coconut

generous ½ cup golden raisins

½ cup candied cherries

Grease and line a 9-inch/23-cm square cake pan. Place the chocolate in a heatproof bowl, set the bowl over a saucepan of gently simmering water, and heat until melted. Remove from the heat and stir until smooth. Pour into the prepared pan and let set for about 1 hour.

Preheat the oven to 350°F/180°C. Cream together the butter and sugar until pale and fluffy. Gradually add the eggs, beating well after each addition. Add the coconut, golden raisins, and candied cherries and stir together until combined. Spoon the mixture into the cake pan on top of the chocolate and spread out evenly.

Bake in the preheated oven for 30–35 minutes, or until golden brown. Let cool in the pan, then turn out and cut into slices.

great tip!
when melting chocolate,
ensure the bottom of the bowl
does not touch the water

Sticky Pecan Pie Bars

Makes 10

½ cup cold unsalted butter, diced, plus extra for greasing

1¼ cups all-purpose flour

⅔ cup light brown sugar

2 extra large eggs

⅓ cup chopped pecans

½ cup dark corn syrup

½ tsp vanilla extract

Preheat the oven to 375°F/190°C. Grease and line a 9-inch/23-cm square cake pan. Grease the paper. Place 2 tablespoons of the butter in a saucepan and heat gently until melted. Let cool slightly.

Sift the flour into a large bowl, add the remaining butter, and rub it in with your fingertips until the mixture resembles fine breadcrumbs. Stir in scant ¼ cup of the sugar, then spoon into the prepared pan and press down firmly with the back of a spoon. Bake in the preheated oven for 20 minutes.

Meanwhile, place the eggs in a large bowl and beat lightly. Add the remaining sugar, the pecans, melted butter, corn syrup, and vanilla extract and stir together until combined.

Pour the mixture into the pan and bake for an additional 15–20 minutes, or until firm to the touch and golden brown. Remove from the pan and let cool. When cold, cut into slices to serve.

Almond & Raspberry Bars

Makes 12

1½ cups all-purpose flour,
   plus extra for dusting

generous ½ cup cold unsalted
   butter

2 tbsp superfine sugar

1 egg yolk

about 1 tbsp cold water

Filling

½ cup butter

generous ½ cup superfine sugar

1 cup ground almonds

3 eggs, beaten

½ tsp almond extract

4 tbsp raspberry jelly

2 tbsp slivered almonds

Sift the flour into a bowl and rub in the butter with your fingertips until the mixture resembles fine breadcrumbs. Stir in the sugar, then combine the egg yolk and water and stir in to make a firm dough. Wrap in plastic wrap and chill for about 15 minutes.

Preheat the oven to 400°F/200°C. Roll out the dough on a lightly floured surface and use to line a 9-inch/23-cm square tart pan. Prick the bottom of the pastry shell all over and chill for 15 minutes.

For the filling, cream the butter and sugar together until pale and fluffy, then beat in the ground almonds, eggs, and almond extract.

Spread the jelly over the bottom of the pastry shell, then top with the almond filling, spreading it evenly. Sprinkle with the slivered almonds.

Bake in the preheated oven for 10 minutes, then reduce the temperature to 350°F/180°C and bake for an additional 25–30 minutes, or until the filling is golden brown and firm to the touch. Cool in the pan, then cut into bars.

Strawberry Chocolate Bars

Makes 16

1⅔ cups all-purpose flour

1 tsp baking powder

½ cup superfine sugar

scant ½ cup light brown sugar

1 cup unsalted butter

1¾ cups rolled oats

⅔ cup strawberry jelly

generous ½ cup semisweet
   chocolate chips

¼ cup slivered almonds

Preheat the oven to 375°F/190°C. Line a 12 x 8-inch/30 x 20-cm baking pan.

Sift the flour and baking powder into a large bowl, add the sugars, and mix well. Add the butter and rub it in with your fingertips until the mixture resembles breadcrumbs. Stir in the oats, then press three-quarters of the mixture into the bottom of the prepared pan. Bake in the preheated oven for 10 minutes.

Spread the jelly over the cooked base and sprinkle over the chocolate chips. Place the remaining flour mixture and the slivered almonds in a bowl and mix together, then sprinkle evenly over the chocolate chips and press down lightly. Bake for an additional 20–25 minutes, or until golden brown. Let cool in the pan, then cut into slices.

variation
replace the strawberry jelly
with apricot jelly

Chocolate Peppermint Bars

Makes 16

4 tbsp unsalted butter,
   plus extra for greasing

¼ cup superfine sugar

generous ¾ cup all-purpose flour

1½ cups confectioners' sugar

1–2 tbsp warm water

½ tsp peppermint extract

2 tsp green food coloring
   (optional)

6 oz/175 g semisweet chocolate,
   broken into pieces

Preheat the oven to 350°F/180°C. Grease and line a 12 x 8-inch/30 x 20-cm shallow baking pan.

Cream together the butter and sugar until pale and fluffy. Stir in the flour until the mixture binds together.

Knead to form a smooth dough, then press over the bottom of the prepared pan and prick all over with a fork. Bake in the preheated oven for 10–15 minutes, or until lightly browned and just firm to the touch. Let cool in the pan.

Sift the confectioners' sugar into a bowl. Gradually add the water, then add the peppermint extract and food coloring, if using. Spread the filling over the base, then let set.

Place the chocolate in a heatproof bowl, set the bowl over a saucepan of gently simmering water, and heat until melted. Spread the melted chocolate over the filling. Let set, then cut into slices.

Chocolate Caramel Shortbread

Makes 12

½ cup unsalted butter,
   plus extra for greasing

scant 1¼ cups all-purpose flour

¼ cup superfine sugar

Filling & topping

scant 1 cup butter

generous ½ cup superfine sugar

3 tbsp dark corn syrup

14 oz/400 g canned condensed
   milk

7 oz/200 g semisweet chocolate,
   broken into pieces

Preheat the oven to 350°F/180°C. Grease and line a 9-inch/23-cm square, shallow cake pan.

Place the butter, flour, and sugar in a food processor and process until they begin to bind together. Press the mixture over the bottom of the prepared pan. Bake in the preheated oven for 20–25 minutes, or until golden.

Meanwhile, make the filling. Place the butter, sugar, corn syrup, and condensed milk in a pan and heat gently until the sugar has dissolved. Bring to a boil and simmer for 6–8 minutes, stirring constantly, until the mixture becomes very thick. Pour the filling over the shortbread and chill in the refrigerator until firm.

Place the chocolate in a heatproof bowl, set the bowl over a saucepan of gently simmering water, and heat until melted. Spread the melted chocolate over the filling. Let set, then cut into bars.

Chocolate Peanut Butter Squares

Makes 20

10½ oz/300 g milk chocolate

2½ cups all-purpose flour

1 tsp baking powder

1 cup unsalted butter, plus extra
   for greasing

1¾ cups light brown sugar

2 cups rolled oats

½ cup chopped mixed nuts

1 egg, lightly beaten

14 oz/400 g canned condensed
   milk

¼ cup chunky peanut butter

Preheat the oven to 350°F/180°C. Grease a 12 x 8-inch/30 x 20-cm shallow baking pan.

Finely chop the chocolate. Sift the flour and baking powder into a large bowl. Add the butter and rub it in with your fingertips until the mixture resembles breadcrumbs. Stir in the sugar, oats, and nuts. Place one-quarter of the mixture into a bowl and stir in the chopped chocolate. Set aside.

Stir the egg into the remaining mixture, then press over the bottom of the prepared pan. Bake in the preheated oven for 15 minutes.

Meanwhile, place the condensed milk and peanut butter in a bowl and mix together. Pour into the pan and spread evenly, then sprinkle the reserved chocolate mixture on top and press down lightly. Bake for an additional 20 minutes, or until golden brown. Let cool in the pan, then cut into squares.

Nutty Oat Bars

Makes 16

2⅓ cups rolled oats

¾ cup chopped hazelnuts

scant ½ cup all-purpose flour

½ cup unsalted butter, plus extra
    for greasing

2 tbsp light corn syrup

scant ½ cup light brown sugar

Preheat the oven to 350°F/180°C. Grease a 9-inch/23-cm square cake pan.

Place the oats, hazelnuts, and flour in a large bowl and stir together.

Place the butter, corn syrup, and sugar in a saucepan over low heat and stir until melted. Pour onto the dry ingredients and mix well. Spoon the mixture into the pan and smooth level.

Bake in the preheated oven for 20–25 minutes, or until golden and firm to the touch. Cut into squares and let cool in the pan.

variation
for fruit and nut bars, add a
handful of chopped dried fruit,
such as dried apricots

Cookies

Chocolate Chip Cookies

Makes 18

½ cup soft margarine, plus extra
   for greasing

1½ cups all-purpose flour

1 tsp baking powder

scant ⅔ cup light brown sugar

¼ cup superfine sugar

½ tsp vanilla extract

1 egg

⅔ cup semisweet chocolate chips

Preheat the oven to 375°F/190°C. Lightly grease two baking sheets.

Place all the ingredients in a large bowl and beat until combined.

Place tablespoonfuls of the mixture onto the prepared baking sheets, spaced well apart.

Bake in the preheated oven for 10–12 minutes, until golden brown.

Let cool for 5–10 minutes, then transfer to wire racks to cool completely.

variation
replace the chocolate chips with chocolate chunks or chopped chocolate

Crunchy Peanut Cookies

Makes 20

generous ½ cup unsalted butter, softened, plus extra for greasing

generous ½ cup chunky peanut butter

generous 1 cup granulated sugar

1 egg, lightly beaten

generous 1 cup all-purpose flour

½ tsp baking powder

pinch of salt

½ cup chopped unsalted peanuts

Place the butter and peanut butter in a large bowl and beat together. Gradually add the sugar and beat well. Add the egg, a little at a time, until it is combined. Sift in the flour, baking powder, and salt. Add the peanuts and bring all of the ingredients together to form a soft dough. Wrap the dough in plastic wrap and chill for 30 minutes.

Preheat the oven to 375°F/190°C. Lightly grease two large baking sheets.

Form the dough into balls and place them on the baking sheets, spaced well apart. Flatten them slightly with your hand.

Bake in the preheated oven for 15 minutes, or until golden brown. Let cool for 5–10 minutes, then transfer to wire racks to cool completely.

variation
sandwich together pairs of these cookies with peanut butter and strawberry jelly

Classic Oat Cookies

Makes 30

¾ cup unsalted butter or
   margarine, plus extra
   for greasing
scant 1⅓ cups raw brown sugar
1 egg
4 tbsp water
1 tsp vanilla extract
4⅓ cups rolled oats
1 cup all-purpose flour
1 tsp salt
½ tsp baking soda

Preheat the oven to 350°F/180°C. Lightly grease two large baking sheets.

Cream together the butter and sugar until pale and fluffy. Beat in the egg, water, and vanilla extract until the mixture is smooth.

In a separate bowl, mix together the oats, flour, salt, and baking soda. Gradually stir the oat mixture into the butter mixture until thoroughly combined.

Put rounded tablespoonfuls of the mixture onto the prepared baking sheet, spaced well apart. Bake in the preheated oven for 15 minutes, or until golden brown.

Let cool for 5–10 minutes, then transfer to wire racks to cool completely.

variation
add ½ cup chopped golden raisins and raisins to the dough

Almond & Raspberry Jelly Drops

Makes about 25

1 cup unsalted butter, softened

scant ¾ cup superfine sugar

1 egg yolk, lightly beaten

2 tsp almond extract

2½ cups all-purpose flour

pinch of salt

½ cup chopped toasted almonds

½ cup chopped candied peel

4 tbsp raspberry jelly

Preheat the oven to 375°F/190°C. Line two baking sheets with parchment paper.

Put the butter and sugar into a bowl and mix well with a wooden spoon, then beat in the egg yolk and almond extract. Sift the flour and salt into the mixture, add the almonds and candied peel, and stir until thoroughly combined.

Scoop out tablespoons of the mixture and shape into balls with your hands, then put them on the prepared baking sheets, spaced well apart. Use the dampened end of the handle of a wooden spoon to make a hollow in the center of each cookie and fill with a little of the jelly.

Bake in the preheated oven for 12–15 minutes, until golden brown. Let cool for 5–10 minutes, then transfer to wire racks to cool completely.

variation
use your favorite jelly in this recipe in place of the raspberry jelly

Date & Lemon Spirals

Makes about 30

1 cup unsalted butter, softened

scant 1 cup superfine sugar

1 egg yolk, lightly beaten

1 tsp lemon extract

2½ cups all-purpose flour

pinch of salt

1⅔ cups finely chopped pitted dried dates

2 tbsp honey

5 tbsp lemon juice

1 tbsp finely grated lemon rind

½ cup water

1 tsp ground cinnamon

Put the butter and scant ¾ cup of the sugar into a bowl and mix well, then beat in the egg yolk and lemon extract. Sift in the flour and salt, and stir until thoroughly combined. Shape the dough into a ball, wrap in plastic wrap, and chill for 30–60 minutes.

Meanwhile, put the dates, honey, lemon juice, lemon rind, and water in a saucepan. Bring to a boil, stirring constantly, then reduce the heat and simmer gently for 5 minutes. Remove from the heat and let cool, then chill for 15 minutes.

Mix together the cinnamon and remaining sugar. Roll out the dough between two sheets of parchment paper into a 12-inch/ 30-cm square. Sprinkle the cinnamon-and-sugar mixture over the dough and roll lightly with the rolling pin. Spread the date mixture evenly over the dough, then roll up like a jelly roll. Wrap in plastic wrap and chill in the refrigerator for 30 minutes.

Preheat the oven to 375°F/190°C. Line two baking sheets with parchment paper. Unwrap the roll and cut into thin slices. Place on the prepared baking sheets, spaced well apart. Bake in the preheated oven for 12–15 minutes, until golden brown. Let cool for 5–10 minutes, then transfer to wire racks to cool completely.

Thanksgiving Cookies

Makes about 30

1 cup unsalted butter, softened

scant ¾ cup superfine sugar

1 egg yolk, lightly beaten

2 tsp orange juice

2½ cups all-purpose flour

pinch of salt

⅓ cup dried blueberries

½ cup fresh cranberries

3 tbsp white chocolate chips

Preheat the oven to 375°F/190°C. Line two baking sheets with parchment paper.

Put the butter and sugar into a bowl and mix well with a wooden spoon, then beat in the egg yolk and orange juice. Sift in the flour and salt, add the blueberries, cranberries, and chocolate chips, and stir until thoroughly combined. Scoop up tablespoons of the dough and put them on the prepared baking sheets, spaced well apart.

Bake in the preheated oven for 10–15 minutes, until light golden brown. Let cool for 5–10 minutes, then transfer to wire racks to cool completely.

variation
replace the fruit with generous ½ cup dried sour cherries and use semisweet chocolate chips

Melting Moments

Makes 32

1½ cups unsalted butter, softened

¾ cup confectioners' sugar

½ tsp vanilla extract

2¼ cups all-purpose flour

generous ⅓ cup cornstarch

Preheat the oven to 350°F/180°C. Line two large baking sheets with parchment paper.

Place the butter and confectioners' sugar in a large bowl and cream together until light and fluffy, then beat in the vanilla extract. Sift in the flour and cornstarch and mix thoroughly.

Spoon the mixture into a pastry bag fitted with a large star tip and pipe cookies onto the prepared baking sheets, spaced well apart.

Bake in the preheated oven for 15–20 minutes, or until golden brown. Let cool on the baking sheets.

variation
dip the cookies into melted chocolate to cover halfway

Fruit & Nut Cookies

Makes 10

½ cup plumped dried apricots

scant ¾ cup all-purpose flour

scant ¾ cup rolled oats

½ cup chopped hazelnuts

generous ½ cup unsalted butter,
   cut into small pieces, plus extra
   for greasing

generous ⅓ cup light brown
   sugar

2 tbsp light corn syrup

Preheat the oven to 350°F/180°C. Lightly grease two baking sheets. Cut the apricots into small pieces using scissors.

Put the flour, oats, hazelnuts, and apricots in a large bowl and stir until thoroughly combined.

Put the butter, sugar, and corn syrup in a saucepan and heat gently, stirring occasionally, until melted.

Pour the melted butter mixture into the bowl and stir to make a soft, chunky dough. Put tablespoonfuls of the dough onto the prepared baking sheets, spaced well apart, and flatten slightly.

Bake in the preheated oven for 15 minutes, until golden brown. Let cool for 5–10 minutes, then transfer to wire racks to cool completely.

Sparkly Stars

Makes 20

1½ cups all-purpose flour,
   plus extra for dusting

1 tsp baking powder

pinch of salt

⅔ cup unsalted butter,
   diced

generous ½ cup light brown
   sugar

1 tsp ground cinnamon

1 egg yolk

edible silver balls, to decorate

Icing

1¾ cups confectioners' sugar

1 tbsp lemon juice

½–1 tbsp water

Preheat the oven to 350°F/180°C. Line two large baking sheets with parchment paper.

Sift the flour, baking powder, and salt into a large bowl. Add the butter and rub it in with your fingertips until the mixture resembles fine breadcrumbs. Stir in the brown sugar, cinnamon, and egg yolk, then mix to a dough.

Roll out the dough on a lightly floured surface to about ¼ inch/5 mm thick. Stamp out cookies with a star-shaped cutter and put them on the prepared baking sheets.

Bake in the preheated oven for 15–20 minutes, until golden brown. Let cool for 5–10 minutes, then transfer to wire racks to cool completely.

To make the icing, put the confectioners' sugar in a small bowl. Add the lemon juice, then gradually stir in the water to make a smooth icing. Spread a little of the icing over each cookie, then decorate with silver balls.

Cherry & Chocolate Diamonds

Makes 30

1 cup unsalted butter, softened

scant ¾ cup superfine sugar

1 egg yolk, lightly beaten

2 tsp vanilla extract

2½ cups all-purpose flour

pinch of salt

¼ cup finely chopped
   candied cherries

⅓ cup milk chocolate chips

Put the butter and sugar into a bowl and mix well with a wooden spoon, then beat in the egg yolk and vanilla extract. Sift in the flour and salt, add the candied cherries and chocolate chips, and stir until thoroughly combined. Shape the dough into a ball, wrap in plastic wrap, and chill for 30–60 minutes.

Preheat the oven to 375°F/190°C. Line two baking sheets with parchment paper.

Roll out the dough between two sheets of parchment paper to about ⅛ inch/3 mm thick. Stamp out cookies with a diamond-shaped cutter and put them on the prepared baking sheets.

Bake in the preheated oven for 10–15 minutes, until golden brown. Let cool for 5–10 minutes, then transfer to wire racks to cool completely.

Vanilla Macaroons

Makes 16

¾ cup ground almonds

1 cup confectioners' sugar

2 extra large egg whites

¼ cup superfine sugar

½ tsp vanilla extract

Filling

4 tbsp unsalted butter, softened

½ tsp vanilla extract

1 cup confectioners' sugar

Place the ground almonds and confectioners' sugar in a food processor and process for 15 seconds. Sift the mixture into a bowl. Line two baking sheets with parchment paper.

Place the egg whites in a large bowl and whip until holding soft peaks. Gradually beat in the superfine sugar to make a firm, glossy meringue. Beat in the vanilla extract.

Fold the almond mixture into the meringue one-third at a time. Continue to cut and fold the mixture until it forms a shiny batter with a thick, ribbonlike consistency. Spoon the batter into a pastry bag fitted with a ½-inch/1-cm plain tip. Pipe 32 small circles onto the prepared baking sheets. Tap the baking sheets firmly and let stand for 30 minutes. Preheat the oven to 325°F/160°C.

Bake in the preheated oven for 10–15 minutes. Let cool for 5–10 minutes, then transfer to wire racks to cool completely.

To make the filling, beat the butter and vanilla extract in a bowl until pale and fluffy. Gradually beat in the confectioners' sugar until smooth. Use to sandwich pairs of macaroons together.

Halloween Spiderweb Cookies

Makes 30

1 cup unsalted butter, softened

scant ¾ cup superfine sugar

1 egg yolk, lightly beaten

1 tsp peppermint extract

2¼ cups all-purpose flour

¼ cup unsweetened cocoa

pinch of salt

Icing

1½ cups confectioners' sugar

a few drops of vanilla extract

1–1½ tbsp hot water

a few drops of black food coloring

Put the butter and superfine sugar into a bowl and mix well, then beat in the egg yolk and peppermint extract. Sift in the flour, cocoa, and salt, and stir until combined. Shape the dough into a ball, wrap in plastic wrap, and chill for 30–60 minutes.

Preheat the oven to 375°F/190°C. Line two baking sheets with parchment paper.

Roll out the dough between two sheets of parchment paper. Stamp out cookies with a 2½-inch/6-cm plain round cutter and put them on the prepared baking sheets.

Bake in the preheated oven for 10–15 minutes, until golden brown. Let cool for 5–10 minutes, then transfer to wire racks to cool completely.

To make the icing, sift the confectioners' sugar into a bowl, add the vanilla extract, and stir in the hot water. Spread most the icing over the cookies. Add the food colouring to the remaining icing and spoon it into a pastry bag fitted with a fine tip. Pipe a series of concentric circles over each cookie, then carefully draw a toothpick through the icing from the center to the outside edge to divide the cookie into eighths and form a spiderweb pattern. Let set.

Vanilla Hearts

Makes 12

1½ cups all-purpose flour,
   plus extra for dusting
scant ¾ cup unsalted butter,
   diced, plus extra for greasing
generous 1 cup superfine sugar,
   plus extra for dusting
1 tsp vanilla extract

Preheat the oven to 350°F/180°C. Lightly grease a baking sheet.

Sift the flour into a large bowl. Add the butter and rub it in with your fingertips until the mixture resembles fine breadcrumbs. Stir in the sugar and vanilla extract and mix together to form a firm dough.

Roll out the dough on a lightly floured surface to about ½ inch/1 cm thick. Stamp out cookies with a heart-shaped cutter measuring 2 inches/5 cm across. Put the cookies on the prepared baking sheet.

Bake in the preheated oven for 15–20 minutes, or until just colored. Let cool for 5–10 minutes, then transfer to wire racks to cool completely. Dust with a little sugar just before serving.

great tip!
place a vanilla bean in your jar of sugar to give it a delicious vanilla flavor

Chocolate-Dipped Viennese Fingers

Makes about 16

scant ½ cup unsalted butter,
   plus extra for greasing

2 tbsp superfine sugar

½ tsp vanilla extract

¾ cup self-rising flour

3½ oz/100 g semisweet chocolate,
   broken into pieces

Preheat the oven to 325°F/160°C. Grease two large baking sheets.

Cream together the butter, sugar, and vanilla extract until pale and fluffy. Stir in the flour, mixing evenly to make a fairly stiff dough.

Spoon the dough into a pastry bag fitted with a large star tip and pipe about 16 fingers, each 2½ inches/6 cm long, onto the prepared baking sheets.

Bake in the preheated oven for 10–15 minutes, or until pale golden. Let cool for 2–3 minutes, then transfer to a wire rack to cool completely.

Place the chocolate in a small heatproof bowl, set over a saucepan of gently simmering water, and heat until melted. Remove from the heat. Dip the ends of each cookie into the chocolate to coat, then place on a sheet of parchment paper and let set.

Alphabet Cookies

Makes 30

1 cup unsalted butter, softened

scant ¾ cup superfine sugar

1 egg yolk, lightly beaten

2 tsp grenadine

2½ cups all-purpose flour

pinch of salt

5–6 tbsp unsalted dried
   pomegranate seeds or
   roasted melon seeds

Put the butter and sugar into a bowl and mix well with a wooden spoon, then beat in the egg yolk and grenadine. Sift in the flour and salt and stir until thoroughly combined. Shape the dough into a ball, wrap in plastic wrap, and chill for 30–60 minutes.

Preheat the oven to 375°F/190°C. Line two baking sheets with parchment paper.

Roll out the dough between two sheets of parchment paper to about ⅛ inch/3 mm thick. Sprinkle the seeds over the dough and roll lightly with the rolling pin. Stamp out letters with alphabet cutters and put them on the prepared baking sheets.

Bake in the preheated oven for 10–12 minutes, until golden brown. Let cool for 5–10 minutes, then transfer to wire racks to cool completely.

Stained Glass Cookies

Makes about 25

2½ cups all-purpose flour,
  plus extra for dusting

pinch of salt

1 tsp baking soda

scant ½ cup unsalted butter,
  diced

1 cup superfine sugar

1 extra large egg

1 tsp vanilla extract

4 tbsp light corn syrup

50 colored hard candies
  (about 9 oz/250 g), chopped

about 25 lengths of ribbon,
  to decorate

Sift the flour, salt, and baking soda into a large bowl. Add the butter and rub it in until the mixture resembles breadcrumbs. Stir in the sugar. Place the egg, vanilla extract, and corn syrup in a separate bowl and whisk together. Pour the egg mixture into the flour mixture and mix to form a smooth dough. Shape the dough into a ball, wrap in plastic wrap, and chill in the refrigerator for 30 minutes.

Preheat the oven to 350°F/180°C. Line two large baking sheets with parchment paper. Roll the dough out on a lightly floured surface to about ¼ inch/5 mm thick. Stamp out cookies with a variety of different cutters.

Transfer the cookies to the prepared baking sheets and cut out shapes from the centers. Fill the holes with candies. Using a skewer, make a hole at the top of each cookie.

Bake in the preheated oven for 10–12 minutes, or until the candies are melted. Make sure the holes are still there, and pierce again if necessary. Let cool on the baking sheets until the centers have hardened. When cold, thread lengths of ribbon through the holes to hang up the cookies.

Gingerbread People

Makes about 20

3¼ cups all-purpose flour,
  plus extra for dusting

2 tsp ground ginger

1 tsp pumpkin pie spice

2 tsp baking soda

½ cup unsalted butter,
  plus extra for greasing

generous ¼ cup dark corn syrup

generous ½ cup dark brown sugar

1 egg, lightly beaten

currants and candied cherries,
  to decorate

Icing

¾ cup confectioners' sugar

3–4 tsp water

Preheat the oven to 325°F/160°C. Grease three large baking sheets.

Sift the flour, ginger, pumpkin pie spice, and baking soda into a large bowl. Place the butter, corn syrup, and brown sugar in a saucepan over low heat and stir until melted. Pour onto the dry ingredients and add the egg. Mix together to form a dough. The dough will be sticky to start with, but will become firmer as it cools.

Roll out the dough on a lightly floured surface to about ⅛ inch/3 mm thick. Stamp out cookies with a gingerbread man cutter and put them on the prepared baking sheets. Decorate with currants for the eyes and pieces of candied cherry for the mouths.

Bake in the preheated oven for 15–20 minutes, or until firm and lightly browned. Let cool for 5–10 minutes, then transfer to wire racks to cool completely.

To make the icing, place the confectioners' sugar and water in a small bowl and mix together. Spoon the icing into a small pastry bag fitted with a fine tip and use to pipe buttons and bows onto the cookies.

Whoopie Pies

Makes 8–10

2 cups all-purpose flour

3 tbsp unsweetened cocoa

1/2 tsp baking soda

1/4 tsp salt

1/2 cup unsalted butter, softened

1 cup light brown sugar

1 egg

1 1/4 tsp vanilla extract

1/2 cup buttermilk

Filling

1/2 cup cream cheese, softened

7-oz/200-g jar marshmallow creme

Preheat the oven to 375°F/190°C. Line two baking sheets with parchment paper.

Sift the flour, cocoa, baking soda, and salt into a large bowl.

In a separate bowl, cream together the butter and sugar until pale and fluffy. Beat in the egg and vanilla extract until thoroughly combined. Stir in one-third of the flour mixture until combined. Add half the buttermilk and stir to mix. Stir in half the remaining flour mixture until combined, then stir in the remaining buttermilk. Finally, mix in the remaining flour mixture.

Spoon the batter onto the prepared baking sheets to make circles 1/2 inch/1 cm high and 3 inches/7.5 cm in diameter. Bake in the preheated oven for 12–14 minutes, until the slightly firm to the touch. Let cool for 15 minutes, then transfer to wire racks to cool completely.

To make the filling, beat the cream cheese in a bowl until light and fluffy. Fold in the marshmallow creme. Use to sandwich together pairs of the circles to make whoopie pies.

Snickerdoodles

Makes 40

1 cup unsalted butter, softened

scant ¾ cup superfine sugar

2 extra large eggs, lightly beaten

1 tsp vanilla extract

3½ cups all-purpose flour

1 tsp baking soda

½ tsp freshly grated nutmeg

pinch of salt

½ cup finely chopped pecans

Cinnamon coating

1 tbsp superfine sugar

2 tsp ground cinnamon

Put the butter and sugar into a bowl and mix well with a wooden spoon, then beat in the eggs and vanilla extract. Sift in the flour, baking soda, nutmeg, and salt, add the pecans, and stir until thoroughly combined. Shape the dough into a ball, wrap in plastic wrap, and chill in the refrigerator for 30–60 minutes.

Preheat the oven to 375°F/190°C. Line two baking sheets with parchment paper.

For the coating, mix together the superfine sugar and cinnamon in a shallow dish. Scoop up tablespoons of the cookie dough and roll into balls. Roll each ball in the cinnamon mixture to coat and put on the prepared baking sheets, spaced well apart.

Bake in the preheated oven for 10–12 minutes, until golden brown. Let cool for 5–10 minutes, then, transfer to wire racks to cool completely.

Jelly Sandwich Cookies

Makes 24

1 cup unsalted butter, softened

½ cup superfine sugar

scant 1½ cups all-purpose flour, plus extra for dusting

pinch of salt

generous 1 cup ground almonds

2 tbsp raspberry jelly

2 tbsp apricot jelly

2 tbsp confectioners' sugar

Cream together the butter and sugar until pale and fluffy. Add the flour, salt, and ground almonds and stir until thoroughly combined. Shape the dough into a ball, wrap in plastic wrap, and chill in the refrigerator for 2 hours.

Preheat the oven to 300°F/150°C. Roll out the dough on a lightly floured surface to about ¼ inch/5 mm thick. Stamp out cookies with a 2¾-inch/7-cm plain round cutter. Use a small round cutter to stamp out the center from half the cookies and put the cookies on two large nonstick baking sheets.

Bake in the preheated oven for 25–30 minutes, or until golden. Let cool for 5–10 minutes, then transfer to wire racks to cool completely.

Spoon the raspberry jelly onto half the whole cookies. Spoon the apricot jelly onto the remaining whole cookies. Top with the cookie rings, pressing down gently, and sift the confectioners' sugar over the tops.

Baked for you with love from:

....

Try these tasty:
....
....
Date made:
....
Ingredients:
....
....

Baked for you with love from:

....

Try these tasty:
....
....

Date made:
....

Ingredients:
....

Baked for you with love from:

....

Try these tasty:
....
....

Date made:
....

Ingredients:
....
....

Baked for you with love from:

....

Try these tasty:
....
....

Date made:
....

Ingredients:
....
....

Yummy !

Try these tasty...
Baked by...

Yummy !

Try these tasty...
Baked by...

Yummy !

Try these tasty...
Baked by...

Yummy !

Try these tasty...
Baked by...

Yummy!

Try these tasty...
Baked by...

Yummy!

Try these tasty...
Baked by...

Yummy!

Try these tasty...
Baked by...

Yummy!

Try these tasty...
Baked by...

Yummy !

Try these tasty...
Baked by...

Yummy !

Try these tasty...
Baked by...

Yummy !

Try these tasty...
Baked by...

Yummy !

Try these tasty...
Baked by...

Yummy !

Try these tasty...

Baked by....

Yummy !

Try these tasty...

Baked by....

Yummy !

Try these tasty...

Baked by....

Yummy !

Try these tasty...

Baked by....